Life in the Word
JOURNAL

by

Joyce Meyer

Harrison House
Tulsa, Oklahoma

2nd Printing

Life In The Word Journal
ISBN 1-57794-046-6
Copyright © 1997 by Joyce Meyer
Life In The Word, Inc.
P. O. Box 655
Fenton, Missouri 63026

Published by Harrison House, Inc.
P. O. Box 35035
Tulsa, Oklahoma 74153

Presented to

_____

By

_____

Date

_____

Occasion

_____

Life in the Word

Dear Friend,

God's Word teaches us that taking time out from our busy schedules to remember and reflect is an important part of strengthening our relationship with God. Remembering is not just a way to learn from mistakes but, more importantly, to reflect and rejoice in the victories God has brought us through.

In Psalm 77:11, 12 (AMP) the psalmist sings:

I will [earnestly] recall the deeds of the Lord; yes, I will [earnestly] remember the wonders [You performed for our fathers] of old.

I will meditate also upon all your works and consider all Your [mighty] deeds.

In the midst of our day-to-day responsibilities, we are often unaware of God's miraculous touches on our lives. Yet, when time gives us the opportunity to reflect on a season of our life, a written journal can make clear when His divine hand guides us and works on our behalf. Our souls are strengthened time and time again by reading our own account of God's unending faithfulness toward us.

For God's children to live from victory to victory, our faith should be strong in Him. I pray that this journal comes to be an exciting record of God's goodness to you and that He may bless and strengthen your faith through it.

God's best to you,

Joyce Meyer

Life in the Word

JOURNAL

Life in the Word

JOURNAL

Life in the Word

JOURNAL

Life in the Word

JOURNAL

Life in the Word

JOURNAL

Life in the Word

JOURNAL

Life in the Word

JOURNAL

Life in the Word

JOURNAL

Life in the Word

JOURNAL

Life in the Word

JOURNAL

JOURNAL

Life in the Word

JOURNAL

Life in the Word

JOURNAL

Life in the Word

JOURNAL

Life in the Word

JOURNAL

Life in the Word

JOURNAL

JOURNAL

Life in the Word

JOURNAL

JOURNAL

Life in the Word

JOURNAL

Life in the Word

JOURNAL

Life in the Word

JOURNAL

Life in the Word

JOURNAL

Life in the Word

JOURNAL

Life in the Word

JOURNAL

Life in the Word

JOURNAL

Life in the Word

JOURNAL

Life in the Word

JOURNAL

Life in the Word

JOURNAL

Life in the Word

JOURNAL

Life in the Word

JOURNAL

Life in the Word

JOURNAL

Life in the Word

JOURNAL

Life in the Word

JOURNAL

Life in the Word

JOURNAL

Life in the Word

JOURNAL

JOURNAL

Life in the Word

JOURNAL

Life in the Word

JOURNAL

Life in the Word

JOURNAL

Life in the Word

JOURNAL

Life in the Word

JOURNAL

Life in the Word

JOURNAL

Life in the Word

JOURNAL

JOURNAL

Life in the Word

JOURNAL

Life in the Word

JOURNAL

Life in the Word

JOURNAL

Life in the Word

JOURNAL

Life in the Word

JOURNAL

Life in the Word

JOURNAL

JOURNAL

Life in the Word

JOURNAL

Life in the Word

JOURNAL

Life in the Word

JOURNAL

Life in the Word

JOURNAL

Life in the Word

JOURNAL

Life in the Word

JOURNAL

Life in the Word

JOURNAL

Life in the Word

JOURNAL

Life in the Word

JOURNAL

Life in the Word

JOURNAL

Life in the Word

JOURNAL

Life in the Word

JOURNAL

Life in the Word

JOURNAL

Life in the Word

JOURNAL

Life in the Word

JOURNAL

JOURNAL

Life in the Word

JOURNAL

Life in the Word

JOURNAL

Life in the Word

JOURNAL

Life in the Word

JOURNAL

Life in the Word

JOURNAL

Life in the Word

JOURNAL

JOURNAL

Life in the Word

JOURNAL

Life in the Word

JOURNAL

Life in the Word